NATURAL DISASTERS

HURRICANES

ABDO
Publishing Company

Rochelle Baltzer

Big Buddy BOOKS
Natural Disasters

VISIT US AT

www.abdopublishing.com

Published by ABDO Publishing Company, 8000 West 78th Street, Edina, Minnesota 55439.

Printed in the United States of America, North Mankato, Minnesota.
052011
092011

♻ PRINTED ON RECYCLED PAPER

Coordinating Series Editor: Sarah Tieck
Contributing Editors: Megan M. Gunderson, BreAnn Rumsch, Marcia Zappa
Graphic Design: Adam Craven
Cover Photograph: *Shutterstock*: Ramon Berk.
Interior Photographs/Illustrations: *AP Photo*: John Bazemore (p. 30), Kike Calvo via AP Images (p. 9), Paul Connors (p. 27), Kevork Djansezian (p. 17), File (p. 15), Eric Gay (p. 19), Vincent Laforet, POOL (p. 25), Israel Leal (p. 7), Wilfredo Lee (p. 21), Craig Lenihan (p. 11), Dave Martin (p. 29), NASA (p. 5), Gary Nichols, US Navy (p. 17), David J. Phillip (pp. 19, 25, 27), David L. Ryan, Pool (p. 15), Lynne Sladky (p. 27); *Photo Researchers, Inc.*: NASA (p. 13); *Shutterstock*: Phillip Lange (p. 23), robootb (p. 25).

Library of Congress Cataloging-in-Publication Data

Baltzer, Rochelle, 1982-
  Hurricanes / Rochelle Baltzer.
    p. cm. -- (Natural disasters)
  ISBN 978-1-61783-032-7
  1. Hurricanes--Juvenile literature. 2. Hurricane damage--Juvenile literature. I. Title.
  QC944.2.B35 2012
  363.34'922--dc22

                              2011013145

CONTENTS

POWERFUL HURRICANES

Above warm ocean waters, storm clouds begin to form. Wind starts to move the clouds. They swirl faster and faster, picking up water and moving toward land. It's a hurricane!

A hurricane is a natural disaster. Natural disasters happen because of weather or changes inside Earth. They can **damage** buildings and land. They can even take lives. By learning about them, people are better able to stay safe.

The name *hurricane* comes from an ancient storm god. In the Caribbean and Mexico this god was known as Hurakan, Huracan, Hunraken, or Jurakan.

Hurricane winds spin around the center of the storm. They move faster than cars on a highway!

WHAT IS A HURRICANE?

A hurricane is a storm that forms over warm ocean waters. Not all hurricanes reach land. But when they do, they bring powerful winds and rain. Sometimes, they lead to other natural disasters such as mudslides.

In parts of the world, hurricanes are called cyclones (SEYE-klohns) or typhoons (teye-FOONS).

BREAKING NEWS

A hurricane is given a man's or woman's name. If it becomes a very damaging hurricane, its name is never used again.

WILD WINDS

For a hurricane to form, conditions need to be just right. About the top 150 feet (50 m) of ocean water must be at least 80°F (27°C). Warm, moist air over the ocean must rise, cool, and turn into clouds.

This leaves warmer, lighter air near the ocean's surface. Then cooler, heavier air moves in. When the warm and cool air meet, they create wind. The wind can begin to swirl. It turns into a storm!

Some hurricanes never make it to land.
They die out over cool ocean water.

9

Some ocean storms stay small. Others keep moving over warm ocean water. Warmth from the ocean strengthens them.

A strong storm swirls faster and faster. When its winds reach higher than 74 miles (119 km) per hour, it becomes a hurricane.

The average hurricane drops more than 2.4 trillion gallons (9 trillion L) of rain per day!

BREAKING NEWS

Hurricanes can last several hours to more than two weeks.

EYE OF THE STORM

Most hurricanes have a hole at the center. This is called the eye. Air inside of the eye is calm. It can even be sunny in the eye.

A band of thick storm clouds swirls around the eye. They form the eyewall. The strongest winds and heaviest rains are in the eyewall.

More bands of thick clouds swirl around the eyewall. They are called rainbands. Rainbands may even have **tornadoes**!

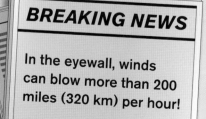

BREAKING NEWS

In the eyewall, winds can blow more than 200 miles (320 km) per hour!

INSIDE A HURRICANE

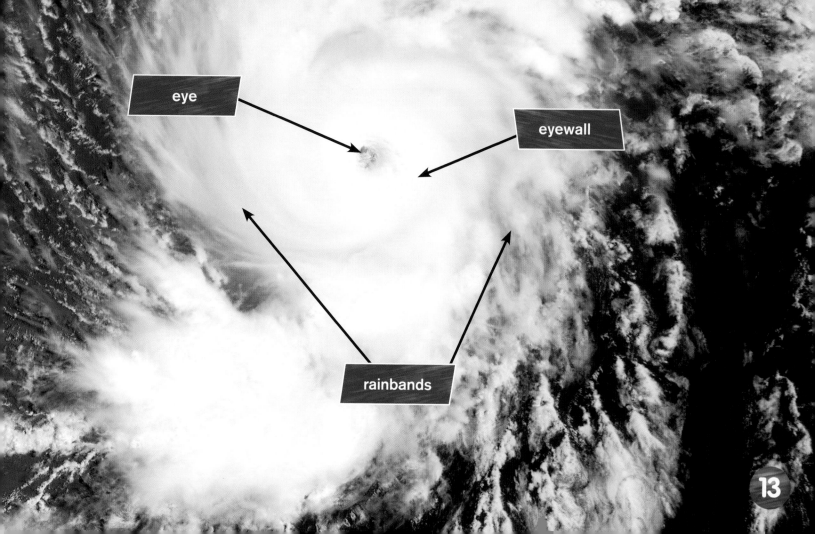

eye

eyewall

rainbands

STORM SURGE

On land, a hurricane's wind can rip off roofs. Pieces of buildings and trees fly through the air.

Wind also causes a rise in sea level called a storm surge. In the ocean, wind pushes the water that is under the hurricane. So when the hurricane hits land, a tall mound of water comes with it.

A storm surge often causes the most harm. It can be more than 20 feet (6 m) high! Sometimes, people and animals get hurt or drown in the water.

In 1900, a hurricane struck Galveston, Texas. Its storm surge killed more than 6,000 people.

A storm surge can be 50 to 100 miles (80 to 160 km) wide.

FLOODS AND MUDSLIDES

A storm surge causes major floods. Heavy rain from a hurricane can also cause floods.

Heavy rain can lead to mudslides, too. When a lot of water falls on a slope, the land can't hold it. It becomes muddy and slips down. The flowing mud can bury buildings, roads, and even bridges!

A hurricane can flood entire towns. People may lose their homes and jobs.

TO THE RESCUE

After a hurricane hits, **rescue** teams get to work. They may use helicopters or boats to bring people to safety. Often, people stay at shelters if their homes have been destroyed.

A hurricane can knock down buildings, power lines, and trees. It can take months or years to clean up. People work together to rebuild areas.

Most of the time, people leave their homes before a hurricane hits. But if they stay, they may have to be rescued.

KEEPING WATCH

Forecasters predict when and where hurricanes will hit. If a hurricane may hit an area within 36 hours, they give a hurricane watch. They give a warning if it is likely to hit within 24 hours.

Scientists measure how strong a hurricane is. They rate its strength on the Saffir-Simpson scale. The scale has five levels based on wind speeds. Category 1 is the weakest, and Category 5 is the strongest.

Hurricane hunters fly into a hurricane! There, they collect data.

Scientists at the National Hurricane Center track storms.

STAYING SAFE

In areas where hurricanes are common, safety measures are taken. Buildings are made to resist **damage**. And, communities have **evacuation** plans.

People who live in these areas listen to weather **forecasters**. They keep safety kits in their homes. If a hurricane is likely, they often board up their windows and leave.

Near coasts, some homes are built on stilts to avoid flood damage from hurricanes. Many have strong coverings to keep windows from being broken.

CASE STUDY:

HURRICANE KATRINA

In August 2005, Hurricane Katrina became a powerful storm in the Gulf of Mexico. When it hit land in Louisiana and Mississippi, it was a Category 4 hurricane.

Hurricane Katrina's fastest winds reached 170 miles (270 km) per hour. Storm surges were more than 26 feet (8 m) high! This led to major floods.

New Orleans, Louisiana, flooded fast. That's because the city was built on very low ground. It had some of the worst damage.

New Orleans had special walls to hold back floodwater. But, Hurricane Katrina was so strong that the walls broke. Can you see the water flowing in?

Hurricane Katrina **damaged** parts of Florida, Louisiana, Mississippi, and Alabama. It was one of the worst natural disasters in US history. About 1,800 people were killed. Many more lost their homes.

People around the country and the world gave their time and money to help. Even today, people continue to rebuild affected areas.

After Hurricane Katrina, it was hard to get food and water. People brought supplies to the survivors.

Flooding water wrecked roads and bridges.

The hurricane left thousands of pets homeless. Rescue workers brought them to places where people could adopt them.

FORCE OF NATURE

Not all hurricanes cause heavy **damage**. But, powerful hurricanes can wipe out entire towns. They can cause floods and mudslides, too.

Scientists continue to study hurricanes. They find new ways to avoid damage and increase safety. Their work saves lives.

A hurricane can tear apart homes and take lives.

NEWS FLASH!

- About 85 hurricanes, cyclones, and typhoons happen each year.

- Florida, Louisiana, Texas, and North Carolina get the most hurricane **damage** in the United States. These states are hit by hurricanes from the Atlantic Ocean and the Gulf of Mexico.

- Most hurricanes are between 100 and 300 miles (160 to 480 km) across.

- Hurricane season happens when ocean water is warmest. In the United States, this is in the summer and fall.

IMPORTANT WORDS

damage (DA-mihj) harm or injury. To damage is to cause harm or injury.

evacuation (ih-va-kyuh-WAY-shuhn) the act of leaving or being removed from a place, especially for safety reasons.

forecaster someone who figures out what is likely to happen by studying facts.

predict to say something is going to happen before it does.

rescue (REHS-kyoo) to save from danger or harm.

tornado (tawr-NAY-doh) a strong wind with a funnel-shaped cloud. A tornado moves in a narrow path.

WEB SITES

To learn more about hurricanes, visit ABDO Publishing Company online. Web sites about hurricanes are featured on our Book Links page. These links are routinely monitored and updated to provide the most current information available.

www.abdopublishing.com

INDEX